SONATINA | *Masterworks*

A series of DYNAMIC *and* VIBRANT *sonatinas*

for performers of all ages

This book is dedicated to Richard Magrath

Cover art: Interior of Saint Peter's, Rome (1735)
by Giovanni Paolo Pannini (Italian, 1691–1765)
Oil on canvas (60 1/4" x 86 1/2")
The Norton Simon Foundation, Pasadena, California

Music engraving: Nancy Butler

Compiled and edited by | JANE MAGRATH

Alfred

Preface

Some of the most rewarding keyboard music for progressing performers is the sonatina literature. Pianists for many years have been drawn to the Clementi *Sonatinas, Op. 36* and to many of those by Kuhlau. *Sonatina Masterworks* Book 3 includes the familiar Clementi *Sonatina in C Major, Op. 36, No. 3*, Benda *Sonatina in A Minor*, Kuhlau *Sonatina in C Major, Op. 55, No. 3* and the Haydn *Sonatina in G Major Hob. XVI:8*. The additional works in Book 3 also come from the standard sonatina literature. This book contains both familiar and well-loved sonatinas as well as several less well-known works of high quality.

The works are included in their entirety. It should be noted that the Benda sonatina is complete in one movement. Dynamic indications, phrase markings and fingerings are editorial. Every effort has been made to retain the highest standard in stylistic articulation and overall performance, while encouraging basic musicality and taking advantage of the capabilities of the modern instrument.

Included in each book is a chart showing a possible order for repertoire study, with pieces listed by individual sonatina movement. Movements of individual sonatinas sometimes vary in difficulty. Some students will complete entire sonatinas, while others may study selected movements from throughout the volume.

Performer's Corner notes for the student are presented at the end of each book. This section contains quick hints to help make these pieces easier to learn and perform. The objective was to isolate one or two central points in each piece to begin the learning process.

I extend warm thanks and sincere appreciation to Morty and Iris Manus and to E. L. Lancaster for their vision, support and help with these volumes.

A Special Note for the Performer

These pieces have been selected with you, the performer, in mind. Every attempt has been made to provide music of the highest quality that will be appealing to you and your audiences. Best wishes for many hours of delight, joy and beauty as you practice and perform these selections. Most importantly, listen carefully to your playing as you practice, and enjoy every piece that you read or study!

Jane Magrath

Suggested Progressive Order for Study

Works are approximately equal in difficulty within a group and are listed alphabetically. Selections in Group A are the least difficult.

GROUP A

Clementi. . . . . *2nd movement from Sonatina in C*
Diabelli . . . . *1st movement*
Gurlitt . . . . *2nd movement*
Haydn . . . . *3rd movement*
Haydn . . . . *4th movement*
Latour . . . . *1st movement*
Latour . . . . *2nd movement*
Latour . . . . *3rd movement*

GROUP B

Camidge. . . . . *1st movement*
Camidge. . . . . *2nd movement*
Clementi. . . . . *1st movement from Sonatina in C*
Clementi. . . . . *3rd movement from Sonatina in C*
Clementi. . . . . *1st movement from Sonatina in D*
Clementi. . . . . *2nd movement from Sonatina in D*
Diabelli . . . . *2nd movement*
Diabelli . . . . *3rd movement*
Gurlitt . . . . *1st movement*
Kuhlau. . . . . *2nd movement from Sonatina in G*
Kuhlau. . . . . *1st movement from Sonatina in C*
Kuhlau. . . . . *2nd movement from Sonatina in C*

GROUP C

Benda. . . . . *Sonatina in A Minor*
Gurlitt . . . . *3rd movement*
Haydn . . . . *1st movement*
Haydn . . . . *2nd movement*
Kuhlau. . . . . *1st movement from Sonatina in G*
Kuhlau. . . . . *3rd movement from Sonatina in G*

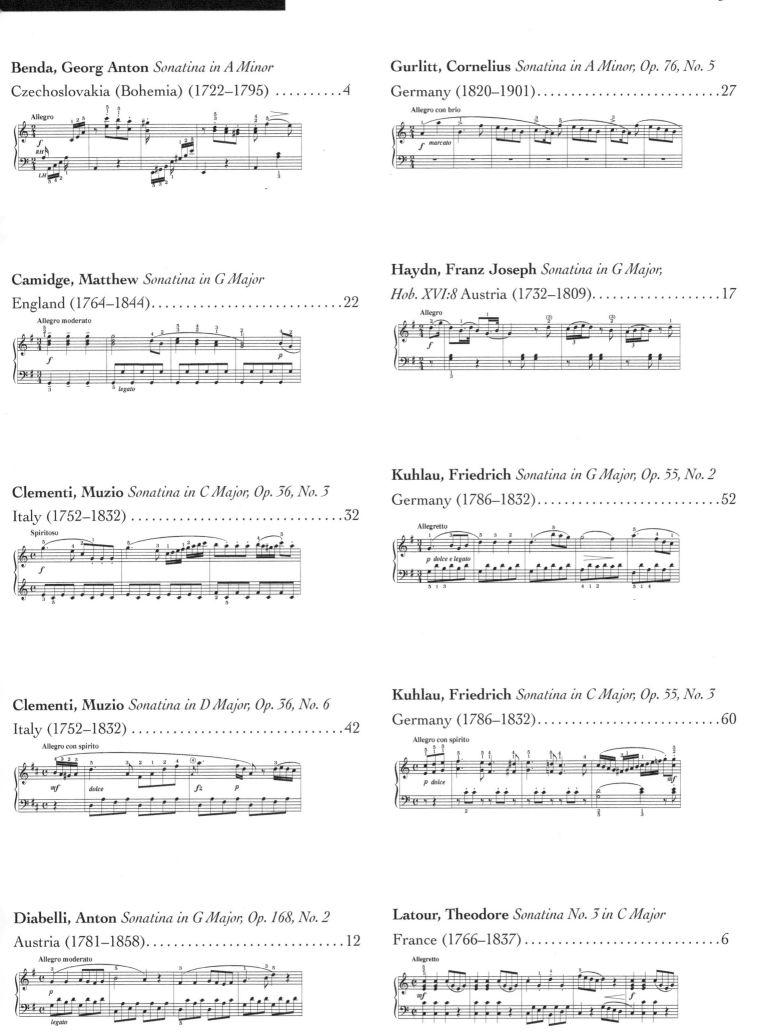

Sonatina in A Minor

Georg Anton Benda
(1722–1795)

D. C. al Fine

Sonatina No. 3 in C Major

I.

Theodore Latour
(1766–1837)

II.

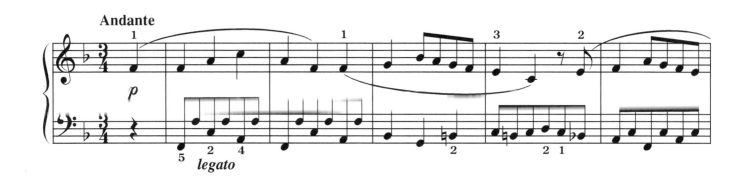

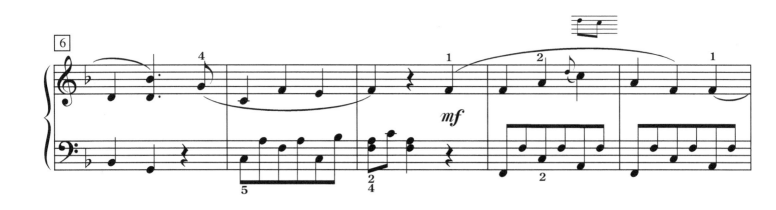

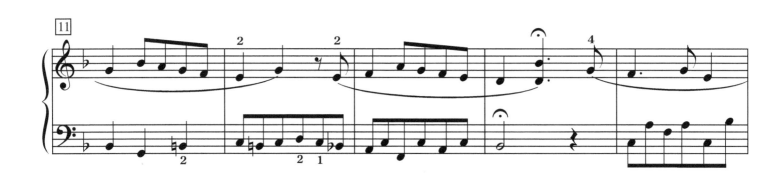

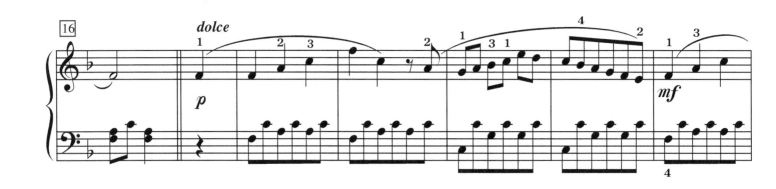

III.

Rondo
Allegro

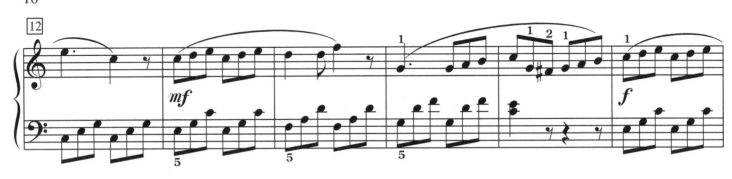

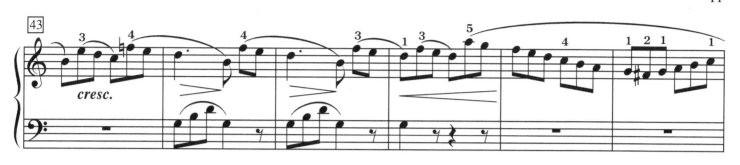

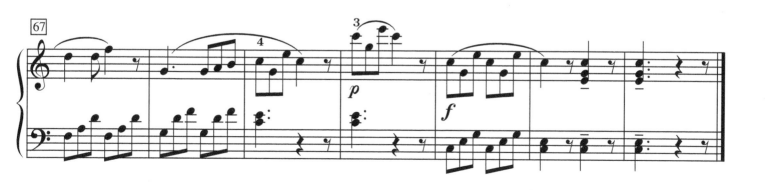

Sonatina in G Major
Op. 168, No. 2
I.

Anton Diabelli
(1781–1858)

II.

III.

Sonatina in G Major
Hob. XVI:8

I.

Franz Joseph Haydn
(1732–1809)

ⓐ A turn may be substituted.

II.

Menuet

III.

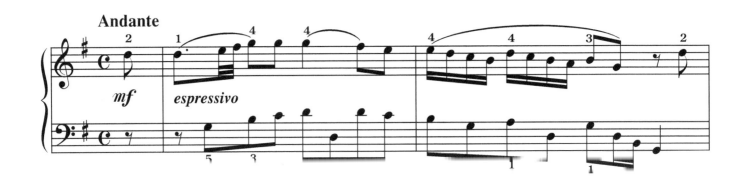

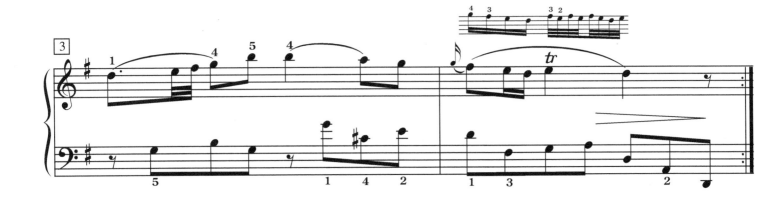

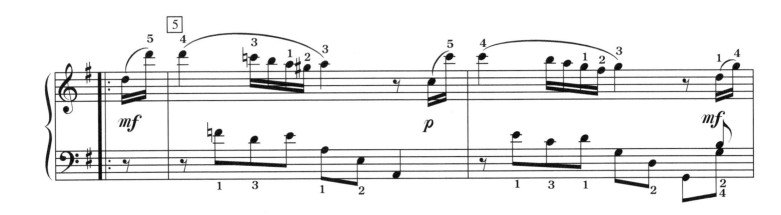

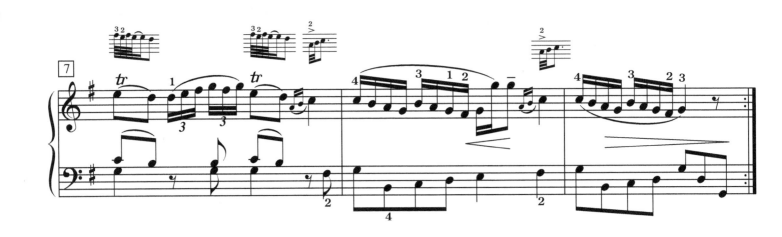

IV.

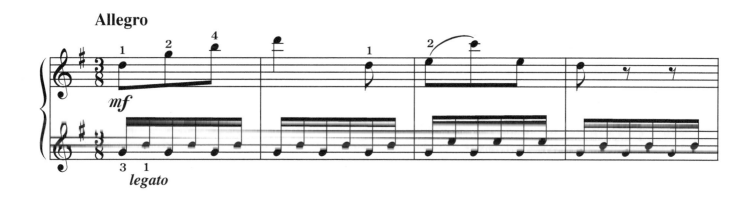

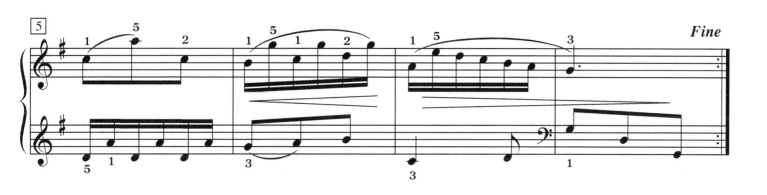

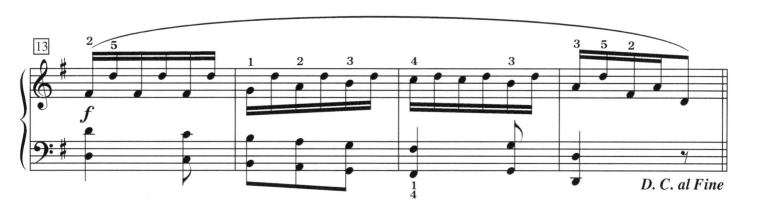

D. C. al Fine

Sonatina in G Major

I.

Matthew Camidge
(1764–1844)

Allegro moderato

II.

Sonatina in A Minor
Op. 76, No. 5

I.

Cornelius Gurlitt
(1820–1901)

II.

Allegretto scherzando

III.

Allegro non troppo

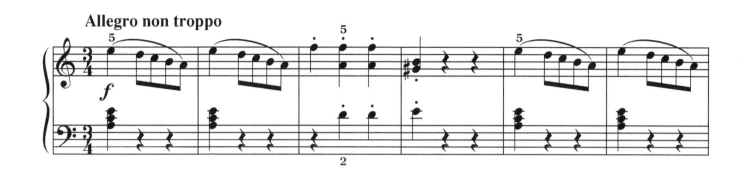

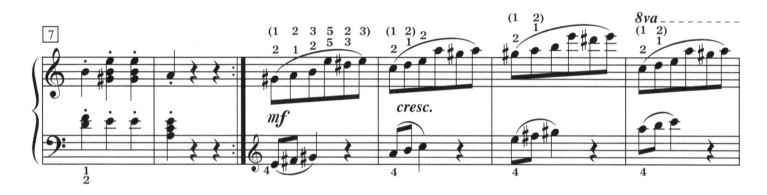

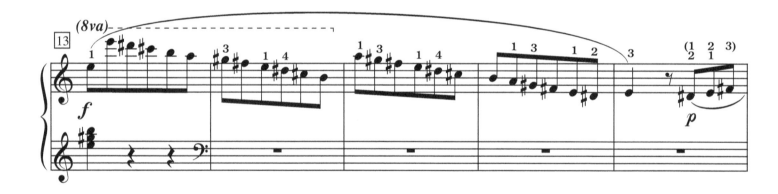

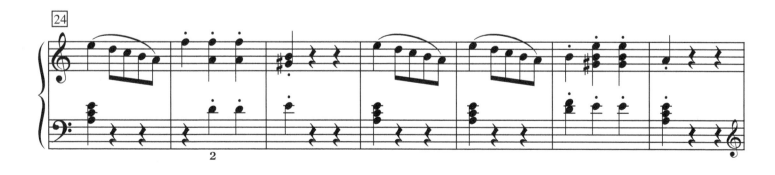

Sonatina in C Major
Op. 36, No. 3

I.

Muzio Clementi
(1752–1832)

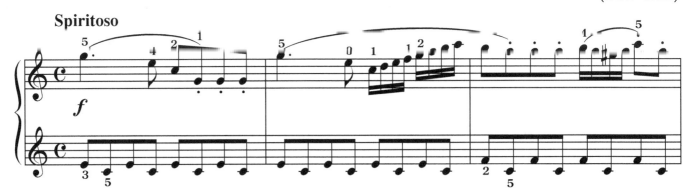

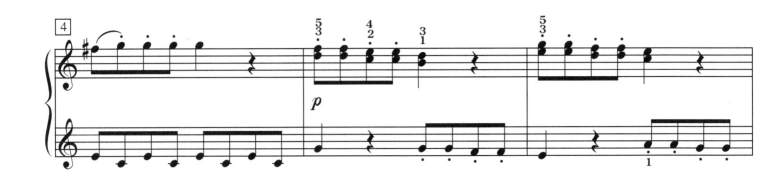

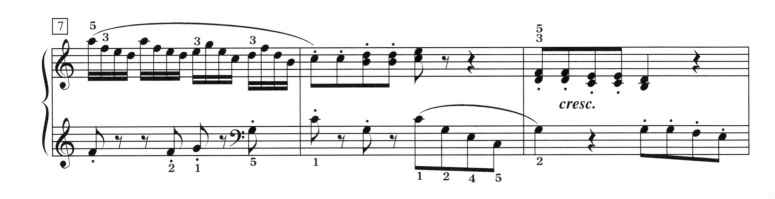

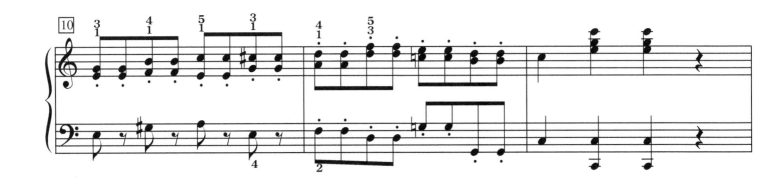

II.

Un poco adagio

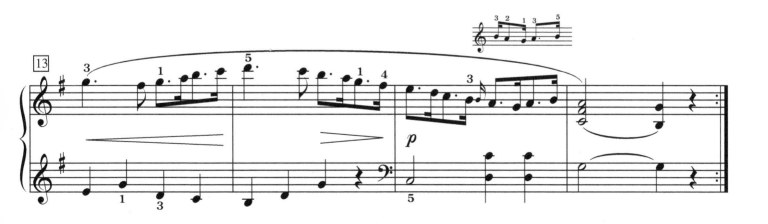

III.

Sonatina in D Major
Op. 36, No. 6

Muzio Clementi
(1752–1832)

Allegro con spirito

ⓐ Play the small note very quickly, on the beat.

II.

ⓐ Play the small notes very quickly, on the beat.

Sonatina in G Major
Op. 55, No. 2

Friedrich Kuhlau
(1786–1832)

ⓐ Play the small note very quickly, on the beat.

II.

III.

ⓐ Play the small notes very quickly, on the beat.

Sonatina in C Major
Op. 55, No. 3

Friedrich Kuhlau
(1786–1832)

II.

Allegretto grazioso

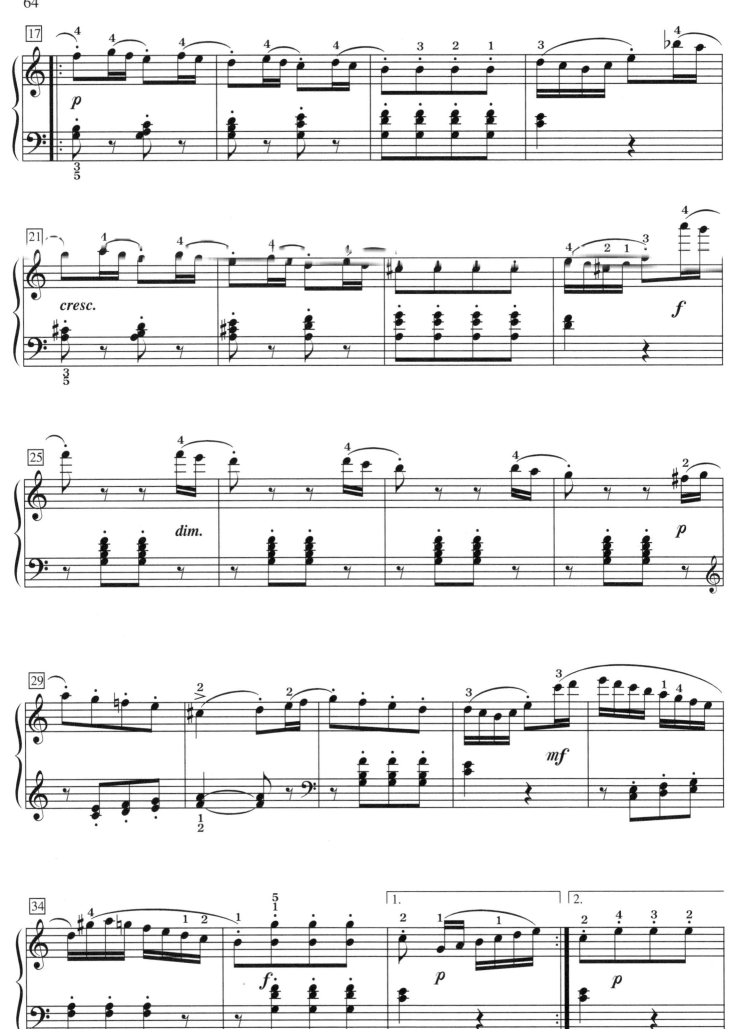

THE PERFORMER'S CORNER

Quick hints to help make these pieces easier to learn and perform.

Benda, Georg Anton *Sonatina in A Minor* 4

- Triads are outlined by the broken chords in many measures.
  Name the triads that are implied by the broken chords in
  measures 1, 3, 8, 17, 19, 25, 27, 33 and 37.

Latour, Theodore *Sonatina No. 3 in C Major* 6

I.   Allegretto
- There is an inflection to the musical line when played well, just as the human voice inflects as one speaks. Sing
  or hum the theme in measures 1–4, and then play, inflecting in a manner similar to that when you sang the theme.
  Follow the same procedure for the theme that begins at measure 10 and for each recurrence of these musical ideas in
  the piece.
- The opening chords represent a fanfare that recurs several times in the movement. Work to bring out the fanfare
  and to project the top note of the chords.

II.   Andante
- The cadenzas in measures 24 and 30 should be played freely and expressively.

III.   Rondo — Allegro
- Circle the word that you feel best fits the mood this piece portrays.

  SAD   POMPOUS   ROLLICKING

- This work has three large sections: A B A. Mark the sections in your music. Notice that the A sections are in the
  key of C while the B section begins in the key of G.

Diabelli, Anton *Sonatina in G Major, Op. 168, No. 2* 12

I.   Allegro moderato
- The melody in this movement is quite lyrical and should be played in
  a singing manner with a very smooth and seamless legato.
- This movement is in sonata-allegro form.
  The *exposition*, measures 1–16, presents the two contrasting main themes. Mark the first and second themes in the
  exposition.
- Does the *development* in measures 17–28 utilize the first or
  the second theme from the exposition?
- What is the key or key area of the theme beginning at measure 8
  in the exposition? What is the key or key area of the theme beginning
  at measure 36 in the *recapitulation*?

II.   Andante sostenuto
• Bring out the top voice of each chord as a melody when you play this movement.

III.   Rondo — Allegretto
• Name and compare the key areas for the sections beginning in
  measures 1, 9, 25, 33 and 45. Using this knowledge of the key areas
  as clues, what is the form of this movement?

Haydn, Franz Joseph *Sonatina in G Major, Hob. XVI:8*

I.   Allegro
• The musical line should be inflected when playing the melody and accompaniment. Sing or hum the motives in
  measures 1 and 2, and then play, inflecting in a manner similar to that when you sang the theme. Follow the same
  procedure for the motives beginning in measures 3–8 and for each recurrence of these musical ideas in the piece.

II.   Menuet
• The melody is based on ascending or descending thirds in many measures in this movement. Which measures of the
  melody are based on thirds?

III.   Andante
• The themes in this piece are repeated, either higher or lower than the original theme. Should the varied theme in
  measure 3 be played more or less strongly than the theme in measure 1? Should the varied theme in measure 6 be
  played more or less strongly than the theme in measure 5?

IV.   Allegro
• Name the intervals used in the sixteenth-note passages in
  measures 1, 3, 5, 9, 10, 11, 13, 14 and 15.

Camidge, Matthew *Sonatina in G Major*

I.   Allegro moderato
• The opening chords represent a fanfare that recurs several times in the movement. Work to bring out the fanfare
  and to project the top note of the chords. Name the measures in this movement where the fanfare reappears after
  measure 1.
• The motive in measure 3 is part of the main theme in this piece.
  Mark the measures in which this motive appears either in thirds or
  sixths throughout the movement.

II.   Presto
• The opening theme is characterized by two staccato eighth notes, repeated on the same pitch. Circle each pair of
  repeated staccato eighth notes in this movement as a reminder to bring out this recurring motive.
• The second part of the theme, four sixteenth notes turning around a single note, recurs throughout the movement.
  Circle each sixteenth-note turn that appears in the movement using a different colored pen.

Gurlitt, Cornelius *Sonatina in A Minor, Op. 76, No. 5*

I.   Allegro con brio
- Compare the statement of the opening theme in measures 1–10 with its repetition one octave lower in measures 11–20. What is the first note in measure 18 that is different from that in measure 8?
- Circle the opening theme and fragments from it used after measure 45.

II.   Allegretto scherzando
- Notice how the composer uses the swaying rhythm (♩   ♪) of the first two measures throughout to create a dance-like feeling.

III.   Allegro non troppo
- How are measures 11 and 12 different from measures 9 and 10?
- What major scale is used in measures 13–16?
- What minor scale is used in measures 56–60?

Clementi, Muzio *Sonatina in C Major, Op. 36, No. 3*

I.   Spiritoso
- In the exposition, the first theme begins in measure 1.
  The second theme in a contrasting mood, key area and character to theme I begins in measure 13. Mark these two themes in your music.
- Compare the motives in measures 1 and 27.
  What is the difference between them?
- A long and exciting passage begins in the development section at measure 42 and continues to measure 48. Which measures of the main theme are used as the basis of this passage?

II.   Un poco adagio
- Notice that the melody in measures 1–2 is inverted or turned upside down in measures 9–10.

III.   Allegro
- Name the triads outlined in the left hand accompaniment in measures 17 through 30. Write the triad name for each measure below the left-hand part in the music.

Clementi, Muzio *Sonatina in D Major, Op. 36, No. 6*

I.   Allegro con spirito
- In the exposition, the first theme begins in measure 1, and the second theme in a contrasting mood, key area and character to theme I begins in measure 23. Mark these two themes in your music. Note that theme I is mostly in the key of D major and that theme II is mostly in the key of A major.
- Listen to the chords and the harmonic outline in measures 45–56.
  Identify the chords and listen for the tension in the harmonic progression.

II.   Allegro spiritoso
- In this movement, the first note (sometimes the first two notes) at the beginning of many measures creates a feeling of tension or unrest. Such occurrences are found in measures 1, 2, 3, 5 and similar places. Circle all points of harmonic tension such as these that you find in this movement.

I.   Allegretto

- Tap and count aloud the right-hand rhythm of the exposition
  (measures 1–20) until it is secure. Continue learning the right-hand
  rhythm of the entire piece securely during the early study of the work.

II.   Cantabile

- Approximately six phrases are presented between measures 1 and 18. Determine whether or not the
  highest note in each of the phrases also is the point of greatest tension or loudest note in each of the
  phrases. Place an arrow above the point of greatest tension in each phrase in this movement.

III.   Allegro

- As you play the scalar sixteenth-note passages in this movement, say aloud the name of the first right-
  hand note in each measure as you play that note. This activity will aid you in stressing the correct
  pulse as you play as well as aid in memorizing the movement more quickly.
- Triads are outlined by the left-hand broken chords in many measures. Name the triads that are
  implied by the broken chords in measures 1–8
  and 41–53. Find other broken chord passages in this movement.

I.   Allegro con spirito

- Listen for two large pulses for each measure in this movement.
  The left-hand eighth notes in measures 1 and 2 and similar places should
  be played lightly.
- How are measures 25–26 different from measures 1–2?
- How are measures 40–43 different from measures 13–16?
- As you play the scalar sixteenth-note passages in measures 46–51,
  say aloud the name of the first right-hand note of each group of sixteenth notes on beats 1 and 3 as
  you play that note. This activity will aid in stressing the correct pulse as you play as well as aid in
  memorizing this part of the movement more quickly.

II.   Allegretto grazioso

- A written out turn (four notes circling a single pitch with step-wise downward and upward motion)
  recurs throughout the movement. It is especially prominent in the B section beginning in measure 38.
  Circle each sixteenth-note turn that occurs in the movement. Be sure to include the turns in measures
  4, 12, 20, 24 and 32 in the A section.
- Many measures in this movement end with three staccato eighth notes
  in both hands (no sixteenth notes). Circle the last three staccato eighth notes in each measures that
  ends only with eighth notes. This recurring rhythmic pattern of three eighth notes unifies the struc-
  ture of the movement for the listener.

LITERATURE LEVELS
for Sonatina Masterworks, Books 1–3

based on
The Pianist's Guide to Standard Teaching and Performance Literature
by Jane Magrath

Book covers are placed to show approximate grading of each volume based on the Level chart from *The Pianist's Guide to Standard Teaching and Performance Literature.*

Level 1	Bartók *Mikrokosmos, Volume 1*
Level 2	Türk *Pieces for Beginners*
Level 3	Latour *Sonatinas*
	Kabalevsky *Pieces for Young People, Op. 39*
Level 4	*Anna Magdalena Bach Notebook*
	Gurlitt *Album for the Young, Op. 140*
	Tchaikovsky *Album for the Young, Op. 39*
Level 5	*Anna Magdalena Bach Notebook*
	Attwood, Lynes *Sonatinas*
	Menotti *Poemetti*
Level 6	Clementi *Sonatinas, Op. 36*
	Burgmüller *25 Progressive Pieces, Op. 100*
Level 7	Kuhlau and moderate Diabelli *Sonatinas*
	Bach easiest *Two-Part Inventions*
	Bach *Short Preludes*
	Dello Joio *Lyric Pieces for the Young*
Level 8	Bach moderately difficult *Two-Part Inventions*
	Beethoven easiest variation sets
	Field *Nocturnes*
	Schumann *Album Leaves, Op. 124*
	Schubert *Waltzes*
	Turina *Miniatures*
Level 9	Bach *Two-Part Inventions*
	Haydn easiest sonata movements
	Mendelssohn easiest *Songs Without Words*
	Chopin easiest *Mazurkas*
Level 10	Bach easiest *Three-Part Inventions*
	Chopin easiest *Nocturnes*
	Beethoven *Sonatas, Op. 49, 79*
	Mozart *Sonata, K. 283*
	Muczynski *Preludes*